THE ART OF CONVERSATION

A GUIDE TO MASTERING THE ART OF EFFECTIVE COMMUNICATION

SUBHASH CHAUDHARY

To my father, who may not be here in person but will always live on in my heart.

As I sit down to write this dedication, tears well up in my eyes as I think about all the memories we shared together. You were my rock, my mentor, my best friend. I feel so blessed to have had you in my life, and I will always treasure the time we had together.

You taught me so much about life, about love, about family, and about the importance of treating others with kindness and respect. You showed me how to be strong, even in the face of adversity, and to never give up on my dreams. You were always there for me, cheering me on, and offering a listening ear whenever I needed it.

I will always remember the way you smiled, the way you laughed, and the way you made everyone feel special. Your presence was a gift to all those who knew you, and you will be deeply missed.

I want to thank you for everything, for all the love and support you gave me throughout my life. I know that you will always be watching over me and guiding me on my journey.

Missing your presence badly, Papa. You will always be loved and never be forgotten.

With all my love and gratitude,

- Your Subhash

Contents

Foreword

The art of conversation is one of the most important skills we can possess in life. Whether it's communicating with loved ones, colleagues, or strangers, our ability to connect with others through words and ideas shapes every aspect of our existence. It's no wonder that some of the most successful people in the world are also masters of conversation.

This book delves into the many nuances of effective communication, offering insights and practical advice on how to improve your conversation skills. From the importance of listening and asking open-ended questions, to managing conflict and building relationships, the author provides a comprehensive guide on how to navigate even the most challenging conversations with grace and poise.

But the book is not just for those looking to sharpen their professional skills. It's also a valuable resource for anyone looking to improve their personal relationships. By learning how to communicate more effectively, we can deepen our connections with loved ones, build stronger friendships, and create a more harmonious community.

I highly recommend this book to anyone looking to improve their conversation skills. It's an essential guide for anyone looking to build stronger relationships and achieve success in both their personal and professional lives.

Preface

The art of conversation is a timeless skill that has been long sought after by people from all walks of life. From kings and queens to college students, the ability to communicate effectively has remained an essential part of human interaction. In this book, I will provide readers with the tools needed to become an effective conversationalists.

This book is divided into three sections: the basics of conversation, the fundamentals of good conversation, and the advanced techniques. In the first section, I will discuss the importance of developing good listening skills, holding a conversation, and understanding nonverbal communication. In the second section, I will focus on the nuances of conversation, such as body language and the power of storytelling. Finally, in the third section, I will explore more advanced techniques, including the art of persuasion, verbal jiu-jitsu, and the power of silence.

By the end of this book, readers will have the skills needed to become an effective conversationalist. Whether you are looking to impress friends and co-workers, or just wanting to feel more comfortable in social situations, this book will provide you with the necessary tools to become a master of conversation.

Acknowledgements

I would like to thank my family and friends for their unwavering support and encouragement throughout the writing of this book. I am especially grateful to my editors, advisors, and readers who have helped me develop and polish this work.

I would also like to thank everyone who has shared their wisdom and insight in the field of conversation, particularly the authors of conversation-related books, articles, and blog posts.

Finally, I would like to express my sincere gratitude to all of the participants of the conversations that I have included in this book. Your stories, experiences, and perspectives have greatly enriched this work.

Prologue

Once upon a time, in a world of endless noise and distractions, an art was lost. An art that was once revered and cherished and passed down through the generations.

The art of conversation

This art was the foundation of relationships, the basis of understanding and a key to unlocking the mysteries of the human condition. It was a skill that had the power to connect and inspire, to bring people together and to build bridges between cultures and societies.

But over time, this art began to fade away. People became too busy and too distracted to take the time to listen and engage in meaningful discourse.

This book is a celebration of this lost art, an exploration of its power, and a guide for regaining it. It is about the power of words, the joy of connection, and the beauty of shared understanding. It is about the art of conversation.

CHAPTER I

Introduction

The art of conversation is a skill that can be developed and improved through practice and effort. It is one of the most important aspects of communication and can be used to build relationships, exchange ideas, and even resolve conflicts. This book is an exploration of the many facets of conversation, from its history and basics to more advanced techniques and strategies.

We will look at the different types of conversations, such as casual conversations, business conversations, and even those that occur online. We will examine the nuances of communication, such as body language, tone, and even the choice of words. We will also discuss the various techniques that can be used to make conversations more meaningful and engaging.

This book is intended to be a guide to help anyone interested in improving their conversational skills. Whether you are a beginner looking to develop your conversation skills, or an experienced conversationalist looking to refine your abilities, there is something here for everyone. With the right knowledge and practice, anyone can improve their ability to communicate effectively and confidently.

CHAPTER II

What is Conversation?

A conversation is an art form that has been practised for centuries. It involves two or more people engaging in an exchange of ideas, opinions, and feelings. The conversation is not just a matter of exchanging words but also involves both verbal and nonverbal communication, such as body language and facial expressions.

When conversing, it is important to be mindful of the other person's feelings and opinions. This requires active listening, which involves paying attention to what the other person is saying and providing feedback and input. The conversation is also a two-way street; it is not just about one person talking and the other person listening. Each person should be able to share their thoughts, feelings, and opinions to foster meaningful dialogue.

To have successful conversations, it is important to be aware of the other person's perspective. This means being respectful and open to different views, even if they differ from your own. Additionally, it is important to be aware of the other person's comfort level, avoiding topics that might be too personal or difficult for them to discuss.

Conversation can be an enjoyable and rewarding experience for both parties. It can help to build relationships, strengthen trust, and exchange ideas. It is a powerful tool that can be used to connect with others and foster meaningful conversations.

CHAPTER III

Preparing for Conversation

The conversation is an art that takes practice and preparation to master. The more you prepare for your conversations, the more successful and enjoyable they will be.

Here are some tips for preparing for conversation:

1. Choose a Topic: Before you engage in conversation, it is important to have a topic in mind. Choose a topic that interests you and the person you are talking to. It should be interesting enough to keep the conversation going but not so controversial that it creates tension.

2. Research: It is important to research before engaging in conversation. This will help ensure that you are well informed and can provide meaningful contributions to the conversation.

3. Rehearse: Rehearsing your conversation can help you feel more confident in the exchange. Rehearsing will also help you think of potential questions or topics you can bring up during the conversation.

4. Be Open-Minded: It is important to be open-minded when conversing. Don't be too quick to judge or make assumptions. Be willing to listen to the other person's point of view.

5. Take Notes: Taking notes during the conversation can help you remember key points or topics. This can help you keep the conversation going and ensure that you do not forget any important points.

By following these tips, you can ensure that you are well-prepared for your conversations. With practice and preparation, you can become an expert conversationalist.

CHAPTER IV

Active Listening

Active listening is an important skill to have when engaging in conversation. It involves being fully present and focused on what the other person is saying. This means not just hearing the words they are saying, but also paying attention to their body language, tone of voice, and facial expressions.

Active listening is a way to show respect and understanding to the person talking. It communicates that you care about what they are saying and are listening with an open mind. It also helps in understanding the speaker's point of view and can help build trust between the two of you.

When engaging in active listening, it is important to keep an open mind and to try not to make assumptions about what the other person is saying. It is also important to avoid interrupting the speaker and to give them the time and space to finish their thoughts.

Active listening also involves asking questions and engaging in a dialogue. This helps to get clarification on the topic being discussed and can help the conversation move forward. It can also help to deepen the conversation by exploring the speaker's views and opinions.

Finally, it is important to provide feedback when engaging in active listening. This can be done through verbal responses, such as saying "I understand" or "That's interesting" or by providing nonverbal cues such as nodding your head in agreement.

Active listening is an important skill to have when engaging in conversation. It allows you to show respect and understanding to the person talking and helps to deepen the conversation. With practice, active listening can become a powerful tool for having meaningful conversations.

CHAPTER V

Starting a Conversation

Conversation is an art. It requires skill, confidence, and practice. It's important to remember that conversation is a two-way street. You have to be willing to both give and receive information if you want to have a successful conversation.

Here are some tips for starting a conversation:

Be positive and enthusiastic. A positive attitude can be contagious and can help you make a good first impression.

Be confident. People generally respond better to someone who appears to be confident. Rehearse what you want to say and practice in front of a mirror.

Start with something simple. Start with a simple greeting or comment if you don't know the person. This can open the door to a deeper conversation. Focus on the other person.

Ask questions and genuinely try to get to know the other person. This will show that you're interested in them and will encourage them to open up.

Listen. It's important to listen actively. Pay attention to the other person and try to understand what they're saying. They'll be more likely to keep talking if they feel like you're listening and engaged.

Be prepared to talk about yourself. Be prepared to talk about yourself, but don't make it all about you. Ask questions about the other person and let them share their story.

Be positive and encouraging. Avoid negative topics and focus on the positive. People generally like to talk about things that make them feel good.

Be prepared to end the conversation. Don't be afraid to end the conversation gracefully if it's going nowhere.

Thank the other person for their time and say goodbye. By following these tips, you'll be well on your way to starting meaningful conversations.

The conversation is an art, but you can become an expert conversationalist with practice and confidence.

CHAPTER VI

Walking into a conversation

When walking into a conversation, it is important to be aware of the context and the people you are engaging with. It is important to remember that the conversation you are about to enter into is an exchange of ideas and thoughts and not a competition.

\When walking into a conversation, it is important to know what you bring to the table. Are you looking to participate in the conversation or make a statement? Are you looking to challenge someone's opinion or to be heard? Knowing your role in the conversation will help you navigate it more effectively.

Before entering into any conversation, it is important to take the time to be an active listener. Listen to the current conversation and consider the context and the tone of the conversation. This will help you to better understand the conversation and to better contribute to it.

When you are ready to enter the conversation, it is important to be mindful of your body language and your tone of voice. Make sure you are making eye contact, maintaining an open posture, and speaking clearly.

When it is your turn to speak, take the time to be thoughtful in your response. Remember that this is a conversation and not a competition. Speak from a place of understanding and respect, and be willing to listen to the perspectives of others.

Finally, it is important to remember to be open to different perspectives and ideas. The art of conversation is about learning from one another, and the only way to do this is to be open to different points of view.

CHAPTER VII

Asking Open-Ended Questions

Asking open-ended questions is a critical component of effective conversation. These types of questions encourage the other person to expand upon their thoughts and ideas, providing deeper insights and a greater understanding of the topic at hand. They also create a sense of engagement and participation, making the conversation feel more collaborative and less like an interview.

One of the most significant benefits of asking open-ended questions is that they help to build trust and rapport. When someone feels that their thoughts and feelings are being heard and valued, they are more likely to open up and share their perspective. This can lead to deeper, more meaningful conversations and stronger relationships.

Open-ended questions typically begin with words like "what," "how," "why," or "tell me about." For example, instead of asking "Are you enjoying the party?" you might ask "What are your thoughts on the party so far?" Instead of asking "Do you like your job?" you might ask "How do you feel about your job?"

Another benefit of open-ended questions is that they allow for more creative thinking and problem-solving. When someone is asked a closed-ended question (one that can be answered with a simple "yes" or "no"), their response is limited to the options presented. On the other hand, open-ended questions allow for a more expansive and imaginative response.

For example, suppose you're trying to solve a problem with a colleague. In that case, you might ask "What do you think we should do?" instead of "Should we do X or Y?" This allows your colleague to come up with their own solutions, rather than being limited to the options you presented.

It's also important to note that asking open-ended questions doesn't mean that you should avoid asking closed-ended questions altogether. There are times when a closed-ended question is more appropriate, such as when you need a specific piece of information or want to confirm something.

For example, if you're planning an event and need to know how many people will be attending, you might ask "How many people will be coming?"

Asking open-ended questions can also be an effective way to diffuse tense or potentially conflictual situations. When someone feels that they are being heard and understood, they are less likely to become defensive or argumentative.

For example, instead of saying "You're wrong," you might say "Can you explain your perspective on this?"

It's also important to listen actively when someone responds to your open-ended question. This means paying close attention to what they're saying, asking follow-up questions, and showing that you're engaged in the conversation.

For example, if someone tells you about a recent experience they had, you might ask "What was the most challenging part of that experience?" or "What did you learn from that experience?"

Asking open-ended questions can also help to build understanding and empathy. When we ask someone about their thoughts and feelings, we gain insight into their perspective and can better understand where they're coming from.

For example, instead of assuming that someone is upset because of something you did, you might ask "What's been on your mind lately?"

It's also worth noting that open-ended questions are not just for verbal conversations. They can also be used in written forms of communication, such as emails and text messages.

For example, if you're trying to get feedback on a project, you might ask "What are your thoughts on the presentation so far?" rather than "Did you like the presentation?"

It's also essential to keep in mind that asking open-ended questions is not a one-size-fits-all solution. It's essential to be mindful of the context and tone of the conversation, as well as the person you're talking to. Some people may be more comfortable with open-ended questions, while others may prefer more closed-ended or direct questions.

For example, if you're talking to someone who is naturally more reserved, you might start with closed-ended questions and gradually transition to open-ended ones.

It's also important to be aware of cultural and social differences when it comes to asking open-ended questions. In some cultures, direct and closed-ended questions may be more common, while in others, indirect and open-ended questions may be preferred.

For example, in some Asian cultures, direct confrontation may be considered impolite, so open-ended questions may be a more appropriate way to address a difficult topic.

Asking open-ended questions is a skill that can be developed and refined over time. It takes practice and patience to become comfortable with this style of communication, but the benefits are well worth it.

Here are a few examples of open-ended questions you can use in different situations:

- In a job interview: "Can you tell me about a time when you had to problem-solve in a difficult situation?"
- In a personal conversation: "How has your day been so far?"
- In a team meeting: "What are your thoughts on the proposal we discussed earlier?"
- In a customer service interaction: "Can you tell me more about the issue you're experiencing?"

In conclusion, asking open-ended questions is a vital tool for effective communication and building strong relationships. By learning to ask open-ended questions, we can encourage deeper conversations, gain a better understanding of other's perspectives, and create a more collaborative and empathetic environment.

CHAPTER VIII

Nonverbal Communication: The Power of Body Language

Nonverbal communication, also known as body language, is an essential component of effective conversation. It refers to the ways in which we communicate through our physical actions, facial expressions, and tone of voice, rather than through words. Research suggests that up to 93% of our communication is nonverbal, making it crucial to understand and master.

Body language can convey a wide range of emotions and messages, from confidence and openness to anxiety and defensiveness. For example, a confident person might stand tall with their shoulders back, while someone who is anxious might fidget or avoid eye contact.

One of the most important aspects of nonverbal communication is the ability to read and interpret the body language of others. This includes understanding the subtle cues and signals that people give off, such as the way they position their body, their facial expressions, and their tone of voice. By learning to read these cues, we can gain a better understanding of what the other person is thinking and feeling.

It's also important to be aware of our own nonverbal communication, and how it may be affecting others. This includes understanding how our own body language, facial expressions, and tone of voice may be perceived by others.

For example, if you're trying to build rapport with someone, you might mirror their body language or make eye contact.

Body language can also be used to build trust and establish credibility. When we appear confident and in control, others are more likely to trust us and believe what we say. On the other hand, if we appear nervous or uncertain, it can undermine our credibility and make it harder to influence others.

For example, if you're giving a presentation, it's important to appear confident and in control, by using a steady voice, making eye contact, and using confident body language.

Nonverbal communication can also be used to influence the outcome of a conversation. For example, if you're trying to persuade someone to see things from your perspective, you might use confident body language and make strong eye contact.

On the other hand, if you're trying to diffuse a tense situation, you might use open, non-threatening body language and avoid crossing your arms or standing in a confrontational stance.

It's also important to be aware of cultural and social differences when it comes to nonverbal communication. Different cultures and societies may have different norms and expectations when it comes to things like eye contact, physical touch, and personal space.

For example, in some cultures, direct eye contact is seen as a sign of honesty and respect, while in others, it may be considered impolite or confrontational.

Nonverbal communication can also vary depending on the situation. For example, the body language and tone of voice we use in a business meeting may be different from what we use in a social setting.

It's also essential to be mindful of the context and tone of the conversation, as well as the person you're talking to. Some people may be more comfortable with direct, assertive body language, while others may prefer more indirect or subtle cues.

Here are a few examples of nonverbal cues and what they may indicate:

Crossed arms: defensiveness or closed-mindedness

Touching the face: uncertainty or dishonesty

Leaning forward: interest and engagement

Avoiding eye contact: discomfort or dishonesty

In conclusion, nonverbal communication, or body language, is a powerful tool for effective conversation. It can convey a wide range of emotions and messages, and its mastery can help us build trust, establish credibility, and influence the outcome of a conversation. Understanding and being aware of our own and others' nonverbal cues can enhance our communication skills and improve our relationships. It is also important to note that nonverbal communication should be used in conjunction with verbal communication, as well as being aware of cultural and social differences.

Nonverbal communication can also change over time, and it's essential to be aware of these changes. For example, if someone's body language becomes more closed off or defensive during a conversation, it could be a sign that they are uncomfortable or disagreeing with what is being discussed.

It's also essential to be aware of the impact of technology on nonverbal communication, as online communication can make it harder to read nonverbal cues. In online communication, we lose many of the nonverbal cues that are present in face-to-face interactions, such as facial expressions and tone of voice.

To overcome this, we can use emoticons, emojis, and other cues to convey emotions and intentions. However, it's important to be aware that these cues are often interpreted differently by different people, and they may not convey the same message as face-to-face nonverbal cues.

In summary, nonverbal communication is an integral part of effective conversation, and its mastery can help us to build trust, establish credibility, and influence the outcome of a conversation. By understanding and being aware of our own and others' nonverbal cues, we can improve our communication skills and strengthen our relationships.

CHAPTER IX

Effective Networking: Building Relationships

Effective networking is the process of building relationships with people in order to achieve professional or personal goals. These relationships can be leveraged to gain access to new opportunities, information, and resources. Networking is an essential skill for anyone looking to advance their career, build a business, or make new connections.

One of the most important aspects of networking is understanding the value of building relationships. The most successful networks are built on trust, mutual respect, and a shared understanding of each other's goals and needs. This means taking the time to get to know the people in your network, and being willing to invest in the relationship over time.

Networking can happen in various forms, such as in-person events, online platforms, or through personal connections. It's important to be open to different forms of networking and to not limit yourself to one specific method.

For example, attending industry conferences and networking events can be a great way to meet new people and make connections, but so can joining online groups or forums related to your industry.

Networking also means being strategic in who you connect with. It's important to focus on building relationships with people who can be valuable assets to your network, such as industry experts, decision-makers, or potential collaborators.

It's also important to be authentic in your networking efforts. Building relationships based on genuine interest and shared values will be more sustainable in the long run.

One key element of networking is the ability to effectively communicate your value proposition. This means being able to clearly articulate what you have to offer, and how you can be of value to the people in your network.

For example, if you're a graphic designer, you might communicate your value proposition by highlighting your ability to create visually compelling designs that help businesses stand out.

Networking also means being willing to give as well as receive. This means being willing to share your knowledge, resources, and connections with others, and to help others achieve their goals.

For example, if you know someone in your network is looking for a job, you might introduce them to someone you know who is hiring.

Networking also means being proactive and following up with the people in your network. This means taking the time to stay in touch, and to reach out to people when appropriate.

For example, if you meet someone at an event and exchange business cards, you might follow up with an email or LinkedIn message a few days later.

It's also important to be aware of cultural and social differences when it comes to networking. Different cultures and societies may have different norms and expectations when it comes to things like initiating contact, building relationships, and following up.

For example, in some cultures, direct and assertive approaches to networking may be more common, while in others, indirect and subtle approaches may be preferred.

Networking also means being aware of the impact of technology on building relationships. With the rise of social media and online networking platforms, it's easier than ever to connect with people. However, it's important to remember that online connections are not the same as face-to-face connections, and they may not be as strong or sustainable.

In conclusion, effective networking is the process of building relationships with people in order to achieve professional or personal goals. It's an essential skill for anyone looking to advance their career, build a business, or make new connections. Building relationships based on trust, mutual respect, and shared understanding is key for successful networking. Networking should be approached strategically, authentically and should include a clear communication of one's value proposition. It's also important to be aware of cultural and social differences, and the impact of technology on building relationships.

It's also important to remember that networking is a continuous process, and not a one-time event. Building a strong network takes time and effort, and it's essential to invest in the relationships you've built. This means staying in touch with the people in your network, offering help and support when needed, and making an effort to maintain the connections.

Networking can also be a great way to learn and grow. By connecting with people who have different experiences and perspectives, you can learn new skills, gain valuable insights, and broaden your horizons.

For example, suppose you're a marketer. In that case, you might network with people in other fields, such as design or technology, to better understand how these fields intersect with marketing.

Networking also means being open to new opportunities. Building a strong network can open doors to new job opportunities, business deals, and collaborations. It's important to be open to new opportunities and to not limit yourself to a specific path.

For example, if you're a writer and you meet an editor at a networking event, you might inquire about the possibility of writing for the publication.

It's also important to be aware of the potential downsides of networking. Building relationships based on superficial or insincere motives can lead to shallow and unsustainable connections. It's important to be genuine and authentic in your networking efforts..

CHAPTER X

The Impact of Technology on Conversation

Technology has had a profound impact on the way we communicate and interact with each other. From social media to instant messaging, technology has changed the way we have conversations and has created new opportunities and challenges for effective communication.

One of the most significant impacts of technology on conversation is the increase in online communication. Social media platforms and instant messaging apps have made it easier than ever to connect with people from all over the world. This has led to a shift in the way we communicate, with more and more conversations taking place online.

However, online communication also has its drawbacks. It can be harder to read nonverbal cues and interpret tone and intent in online conversations. This can lead to misunderstandings and miscommunication.

Another impact of technology on conversation is the increase in multitasking. With the rise of smartphones and other mobile devices, it's now easier than ever to multitask while having a conversation. This can be a distraction and can lead to a lack of focus and engagement in the conversation.

Technology has also led to the rise of virtual conversations and communication. Platforms like Zoom, Skype, and Google Meet have made it possible to have conversations with people in different locations, in real-time, and has allowed businesses to conduct meetings and interviews remotely.

However, virtual communication also has its challenges, such as internet connectivity issues, delays, and lack of non-verbal cues.

Another way technology has impacted conversation is the rise of messaging apps and chatbots. These tools allow for quick and easy communication, but can also lead to a lack of personal touch and human interaction.

Technology has also had an impact on the way we express emotions and convey meaning. Emoticons, emojis, and other cues have become an integral part of online communication, but their meaning can be interpreted differently by different people.

Additionally, the rise of artificial intelligence and machine learning has led to the development of chatbots, which can simulate human conversation. However, these AI-powered chatbots can't fully replicate human emotions and empathy.

In conclusion, technology has had a significant impact on the way we communicate and interact with each other. While technology has created new opportunities for conversation, it's important to be aware of its drawbacks and to make an effort to maintain human connections and interactions.

CHAPTER XI

Cultural Competence in Conversation

Cultural competence refers to the ability to understand, appreciate, and effectively communicate with people from different cultural backgrounds. In today's globalized world, cultural competence is an essential skill for effective communication and building strong relationships.

Cultural competence in conversation means being aware of and sensitive to cultural differences in communication styles, norms, and expectations. It also means being open-minded and willing to learn about other cultures.

For example, in some cultures, direct and assertive communication is considered appropriate, while in others, indirect and subtle communication may be preferred. It's important to be aware of these cultural differences and to adapt your communication style accordingly.

Cultural competence also means being aware of the impact of language on communication. Different cultures have different languages, and language barriers can create challenges in communication. It's important to be aware of these barriers and to make an effort to overcome them.

For example, if you're communicating with someone who speaks a different language, you might use an interpreter or use translation software.

Cultural competence also means being aware of the impact of nonverbal communication on conversation. Different cultures have different norms and expectations when it comes to things like eye contact, physical touch, and personal space. It's important to be aware of these cultural differences and to adapt your nonverbal communication accordingly.

For example, in some cultures, direct eye contact is seen as a sign of honesty and respect, while in others, it may be considered impolite or confrontational.

It's also important to be aware of cultural and social differences when it comes to topics of conversation. Different cultures have different norms and expectations when it comes to discussing sensitive or taboo topics. It's important to be aware of these cultural differences and to avoid discussing sensitive topics if it makes the other person uncomfortable.

Cultural competence also means being aware of the impact of stereotypes and biases on conversation. Stereotypes and biases can create challenges in communication, and it's important to be aware of them and to make an effort to overcome them.

For example, if you're communicating with someone from a different culture, it's important to avoid making assumptions about their background or beliefs based on stereotypes or biases.

Cultural competence also means being aware of the impact of privilege on conversation. Privilege refers to some individuals' advantages and benefits based on their social identity. It's important to be aware of one's privilege and to use it responsibly in conversation. For example, suppose you are from a dominant culture. In that case, it's important to be mindful of the power dynamics in the conversation and to not speak over or dominate the conversation with people from marginalized cultures.

Cultural competence also means being aware of the impact of power dynamics on conversation. Different cultures have different power structures and hierarchies, and it's important to be aware of these dynamics and to communicate accordingly.

For example, in some cultures, it's important to show respect to elders and those in positions of authority, while in others, it's important to challenge authority and speak up for oneself.

In summary, cultural competence in conversation is the ability to understand, appreciate, and effectively communicate with people from different cultural backgrounds. It's essential to be aware of cultural differences in communication styles, norms, and expectations and to make an effort to overcome language barriers, biases, power dynamics and privilege in conversation. It's important to be open-minded and willing to learn about other cultures and to adapt one's communication style accordingly.

CHAPTER XII

The Role of Empathy in Conversation

Empathy refers to the ability to understand and share the feelings of others. It's a crucial component of effective communication and is essential for building strong relationships. In a conversation, empathy allows us to connect with others on a deeper level and to understand their perspective.

Empathy in conversation means being able to put oneself in the other person's shoes and to understand their emotions and thoughts. It also means being able to respond to their emotions and thoughts in a way that is appropriate and supportive.

For example, if someone is sharing a difficult experience with you, empathy would involve being able to understand and validate their feelings, rather than dismissing or minimizing them.

Empathy also means being able to communicate in a way that is nonjudgmental and supportive. This means avoiding criticism or blame and instead, focusing on understanding and supporting the other person.

For example, if someone is sharing a difficult experience, empathy would involve being able to listen without judgment and to offer support and understanding.

Empathy also means being able to communicate in a way that is sensitive to the other person's emotional state. This means being able to read nonverbal cues and to respond appropriately.

For example, if someone is upset, empathy would involve being able to respond in a way that is calming and supportive, rather than exacerbating the situation.

Empathy also means being able to communicate in a way that is respectful of the other person's boundaries. This means being able to respect their right to privacy and to not push them to share more than they are comfortable with.

Empathy also means being able to communicate in a way that is authentic and genuine. This means being able to be present in the conversation and to not fake or feign empathy.

Empathy also means being able to communicate in a way that is inclusive and respectful of diversity. This means being able to understand and appreciate the unique perspectives and experiences of different cultures and backgrounds.

Empathy also means being able to communicate in a way that is aware of power dynamics. This means being aware of one's own privilege and the impact it has on the conversation and being able to navigate these dynamics with respect and understanding.

Empathy also means being able to communicate in a way that is aware of one's own emotions. This means being able to regulate one's own emotions and to not let them negatively impact the conversation.

In summary, empathy is the ability to understand and share the feelings of others, and it's a crucial component of effective communication. Empathy in conversation means being able to put oneself in the other person's shoes, to communicate in a nonjudgmental and supportive way, to be sensitive to the other person's emotional state, to respect boundaries, to be authentic and genuine, inclusive, aware of power dynamics and one's own emotions. Empathy allows us to connect with others on a deeper level and to understand their perspective.

CHAPTER XIII

Intimate Fishing

The art of conversation is an important skill to cultivate in any relationship. People often overlook the importance of this skill in their relationships, but it is an important part of a healthy and successful relationship. Intimate fishing is a way to practice the art of conversation in a more meaningful way.

Intimate fishing is a way to engage in conversations that are more meaningful and personal in nature. Rather than just discussing the day's events or the weather, intimate fishing focuses on more personal and revealing topics.

This type of conversation encourages people to open up and share details about themselves, their values, and their goals.

When engaging in intimate fishing, it is important to be aware of the other person's feelings and boundaries. People should feel secure in being able to share personal details without being judged or criticized. There should be a sense of safety and security in the conversation so that people are not afraid to open up and share.

Intimate fishing can be done in a variety of ways. It can be done one-on-one, in a group setting, or even over text or video chat. People can take turns asking questions and discussing topics that they find interesting or important. The purpose of intimate fishing is to create a space in which people can be more honest and open with each other.

Intimate fishing can be used as a tool to deepen relationships by creating a space for meaningful conversations. As people become more comfortable with each other, they will be more likely to open up and share personal details about themselves. This creates a deeper and more meaningful connection between two people.

Intimate fishing can be a great way to build trust in a relationship. It allows people to get to know each other better, which can lead to a more trusting and deeper connection. Intimate fishing can also be used to practice the art of conversation and to become better communicators.

The art of conversation is an important skill to cultivate in any relationship. Intimate fishing is a great tool to practice the art of conversation in a more meaningful and intimate way. People can use this tool to deepen relationships and create a more trusting and meaningful connection between two people.

CHAPTER XIV

Understanding Your Opponent

One of the most important skills of the art of conversation is understanding your opponent. Whether you are in a debate, a discussion, or simply a casual chat, understanding your opponent is key to having a successful conversation. Knowing and understanding your opponent will help you better connect and engage with them, as well as help you better anticipate their responses and position your own arguments.

The first step in understanding your opponent is to listen carefully and attentively. Take the time to really hear what they are saying, not just hear the words they are saying, but also what they are trying to communicate. Pay attention to their tone and body language. Look for clues that can tell you more about their thoughts and feelings.

Secondly, ask questions. Asking questions is a great way to gain insights and learn more about your opponent. It shows them that you are genuinely interested in what they say and can help you better understand their perspective. However, it is important to keep your questions open-ended and avoid asking leading questions.

Thirdly, try to see things from their perspective. Take the time to consider and understand their point of view. Think about why they might feel the way they do, and even if you don't agree with them, show them respect by acknowledging their perspective.

Finally, be willing to compromise. When engaging in a conversation, it is important to be open to different points of view, be willing to compromise, and be ready to adjust your own stance if necessary. Be willing to work together to find a solution that works for both of you.

By taking the time to understand your opponent, you can create a strong connection and more meaningful conversations. So take the time to get to know them and show them that you are listening and that you care about what they have to say.

CHAPTER XV

Comfort

25

Comfort is an important part of any conversation. It is not only important to make the other person feel comfortable, but it is also an important part of making the conversation flow smoothly and naturally.

One of the best ways to make a person feel comfortable is to show interest in what they are saying. This can be done through active listening, giving appropriate responses and showing that you understand what they are saying.

Additionally, being open and honest with your thoughts and feelings is important. This will help to create an atmosphere of trust and understanding.

Another way to create a comfortable atmosphere is to use humour. Humour can be a great tool to break the ice and break down any potential barriers. However, it is important to be aware of the other person's sense of humour and not use humour in a way that could be seen as offensive.

Finally, it is important to maintain a relaxed and friendly tone. This can be done through body language, such as smiling, maintaining eye contact, and using an appropriate volume. Additionally, it is important to not take the conversation too seriously and to not be judgmental.

By following these tips, you can create a comfortable environment that will help the conversation flow naturally and easily.

CHAPTER XVI

Demanding what you want

When it comes to conversations, there are times when it's appropriate to demand what you want. This could be in a professional setting, where it's expected that you'll be assertive in getting your point across, or in a personal setting, where you may need to be firm in order to get the outcome you desire.

Learning how to effectively demand what you want is an important part of having successful conversations.

Here are some tips to help you do just that.

1. Be Clear and Direct: When you're making a demand, it's important to be clear and direct. Be sure to state your expectations and the outcome you desire. Avoid leaving room for misinterpretation or misunderstanding.

2. Speak With Confidence: Speak with confidence when making your demand. Don't be apologetic or hesitant. This will make it clear that you expect your demand to be met.

3. Listen to the Other Person: When making your demand, it's important to listen to the other person's response. They may have a valid reason for not being able to comply with your request. If this is the case, be open to discussing the issue further.

4. Be Prepared to Negotiate: In some cases, it may be necessary to negotiate in order to get what you want. Be prepared to compromise and give the other person something in return for meeting your demand.

Learning to effectively demand what you want is an important part of successful conversations. Be clear and direct, speak confidently, listen to the other person, and be prepared to negotiate. With these tips, you'll be able to get the outcome you desire in any conversation.

CHAPTER XVII

Mastering Small Talk and Building Rapport

Small talk refers to casual conversation that takes place in social or professional settings. It's often seen as an essential part of building relationships and can be used to establish a connection and create a sense of rapport. Mastering small talk is an important skill for effective communication and building strong relationships.

Building rapport in a conversation means creating a sense of connection and understanding with the other person. It's important to establish rapport to ensure that the conversation flows smoothly and that both parties feel comfortable and at ease.

One way to establish rapport in a conversation is to use open-ended questions. These are questions that encourage the other person to talk and share more about themselves. Open-ended questions can also be used to steer the conversation towards a common interest or topic.

Another way to establish rapport in a conversation is to actively listen. This means giving the other person your full attention and showing that you are interested in what they have to say. It also means being able to reflect back what they said, to show that you understand and heard them.

It's also important to be aware of nonverbal cues when building rapport. This means being aware of body language, facial expressions, and tone of voice, to ensure that the conversation is flowing smoothly.

Another way to build rapport is to use humor. Humor can be used to lighten the mood and to make the conversation more enjoyable. However, it's important to be aware of cultural differences when using humor and to ensure that it's not offensive or insensitive.

It's also important to be aware of cultural and social differences when building rapport. Different cultures and societies may have different norms and expectations when it comes to things like initiating conversation, building relationships, and following up. It's important to be aware of these cultural differences and to adapt your communication style accordingly.

Another important aspect of building rapport is being aware of and managing one's own emotions. This means being able to regulate one's own emotions, to not let them negatively impact the conversation and to not take things too personally.

Also, it's important to be aware of the impact of one's own biases and stereotypes on the conversation. These unconscious biases can create challenges in building rapport and it's important to be aware of them and to make an effort to overcome them.

Another way to build rapport is by finding common ground. This means identifying shared interests, experiences or values that you can talk about and connect over. This can help to create a sense of mutual understanding and can be a powerful tool in building rapport.

In addition, showing genuine interest and curiosity in the other person can be a powerful tool to build rapport. People appreciate when someone is genuinely interested in them and their experiences. It makes them feel valued and important.

It's also important to be aware of the impact of technology on building rapport. Social media and messaging apps have made it easier than ever to connect with others, but it's important to remember that building rapport requires face-to-face interactions and personal touch.

In summary, mastering small talk and building rapport is essential for effective communication and building strong relationships. Building rapport means creating a sense of connection and understanding with the other person, using open-ended questions, actively listening, being aware of nonverbal cues, using humor, being aware of cultural and social differences, managing one's own emotions, overcoming biases and stereotypes, finding common ground, showing genuine interest and being aware of the impact of technology on building rapport.

CHAPTER XVIII

Ending a Conversation

The art of conversation is an invaluable skill, and mastering the art of ending a conversation is just as important as any other aspect of conversation. Knowing how to end a conversation gracefully can be the difference between a successful meeting and a disaster.

When it comes to ending a conversation, it is important to be mindful of the other person and their feelings. Ideally, you should take the time to thank the other person for their time and express your appreciation for the conversation. It is also important to make sure that you don't leave the other person hanging, and that you have settled any unresolved issues.

One of the most effective ways to end a conversation is to summarize the conversation and ask the other person if they have any questions or comments. This allows the other person to feel heard and understood, and allows you to make sure that you haven't left anything unanswered.

If the conversation has been particularly long, it can be helpful to set a deadline for when the conversation should end. This can be done by setting a time limit, or by simply telling the other person that you need to wrap up the conversation soon.

Finally, it is important to remember to stay polite and courteous during the end of the conversation. Don't be too abrupt or aggressive, and don't be afraid to offer the other person a handshake or hug if it feels appropriate.

By following these tips, you can ensure that your conversations end gracefully and that both parties feel satisfied with the conversation. With practice, you will be able to master the art of ending a conversation, and you will be able to make sure that every conversation you have is a successful one.

The Power Of Conversation

Conversation is a powerful tool. It is the art of connecting with people and building relationships. It is a way of expressing yourself, your thoughts, and your feelings. It is a way of connecting to people on a deeper level than just words.

When done right, conversation has the power to create lasting bonds and open up new possibilities.

Conversation is a skill that can be learned. It takes practice and patience, but with the right approach it can be mastered. When engaging in conversation, it is important to remember to be present in the moment and listen to what the other person has to say.

Listening is a vital part of effective communication and it is essential to have good listening skills in order to have meaningful conversations. In addition to listening, it is also important to be mindful of the language you use. Choose your words carefully and be mindful of how they will be interpreted. It is also important to be aware of your body language and the non-verbal cues you are sending to the other person.

The power of conversation lies in its ability to bring people together, build relationships, and create understanding. If used correctly, it can be a powerful tool to foster connection, build trust, and explore new possibilities. So, the next time you find yourself engaging in a conversation, remember the power of conversation and use it to create something special.